Your own wellness

Everyone has the opportunity to be active participants in the care and maintenance of their own wellness, whether it is physical, psychological, social or spiritual.

While the severity of chronic health problems like heart disease, diabetes, hypertension and asthma are determined in part by the quality of health care you receive, there are lifestyle and habit changes you can make to benefit your own long-term physical health. The same is true for your mental health.

Your health is in your hands, and promoting it is a partnership between you and your health care providers.

Within the past few decades, an enormous amount has been learned about human psychology and addiction. The purpose of this Journal is to provide you with some of that knowledge and to help you apply it to the rest of your life.

Wholeness

Your psychological health is closely related to the rest of your health. Mental health is affected by the state of your physical body, your relationships and your spirituality. Drug and alcohol problems can alter each of these areas of your health. This Journal focuses on psychological wellness.

You are a whole person in body, mind and spirit.

© 2010 The Change Companies®

What is...

Mental health is your own current state of psychological wellness. It can change from day to day, like the weather. Unlike the weather, there are plenty of ways to influence and strengthen your mental health. Just as healthy eating and exercise can improve your physical health, there are things you can do on a regular basis to guide yourself toward optimal mental health.

While there are many ways to think about mental health, there are at least three common dimensions to consider. The psychological names for these are as easy as A-B-C: **Affect, Behavior** and **Cognition**.

AFFECT *refers to your feelings and emotions, such as anger, joy, fear, love and sadness.*

BEHAVIOR *refers to your actions, the things you do.*

COGNITION *refers to your thoughts, how you think about things.*

"They'd ask me, 'Why did you do that?' and I'd say, 'I don't know.' There was always a reason, but I didn't know myself well enough to understand what it was."

...mental health?

As you will see later on in this Journal, these three dimensions are closely linked. What you think influences how you feel and what you do. What you do influences how you think and feel. How you feel influences your thoughts and actions.

See how they all connect? This is good – it means that making a positive change in any one of these areas is likely to benefit the others as well.

Describe a time when your thoughts influenced how you felt and what you did.

How would you change...

Whether you are being treated by health professionals or working on your own, it is important to know what you are working toward. How would you most like your life to be different from how it is now? If you could wave a wand and magically change yourself and your life to be how you would like, what would be different? To begin with, think about the three aspects of your mental health mentioned on page 2.

What concerns do you have about your AFFECT? What changes would you like to see in how you feel – your emotions?

What concerns do you have about your BEHAVIOR? What changes would you like to see in what you do, the way you act?

What concerns do you have about your COGNITION? What changes would you like to see in how you think, what you think about?

...if you could?

Here are some changes that people would sometimes like to make in their lives. For each one, put a check mark (✔) to indicate whether it is something you may want to change.

	No	Maybe	Yes	Definitely
I want to be a better parent.				
I want to improve my physical health.				
I want to decrease stress and tension in my life.				
I want to be more physically fit and strong.				
I want to manage my anger better.				
I want to stop smoking.				
I want to improve my marriage/relationships.				
I want to cut down or quit drinking alcohol.				
I want to cut down or quit using other drugs.				
I want to get motivated for change.				

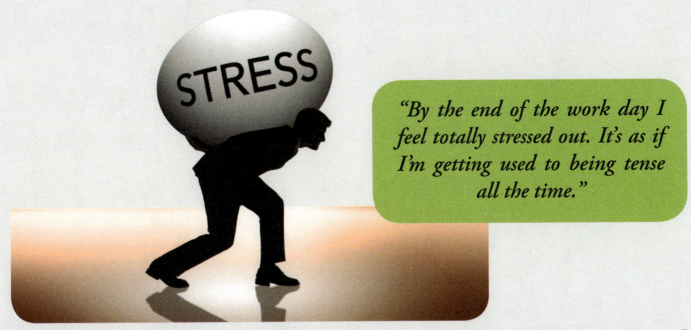

"By the end of the work day I feel totally stressed out. It's as if I'm getting used to being tense all the time."

More or less?

Next think in terms of what you might want **MORE** or **LESS** of in your life and in yourself.

I would like to be more...
_____
_____
_____
_____
_____
_____
_____
_____
_____

I want to experience or do MORE of these things:
_____
_____
_____
_____
_____
_____
_____
_____
_____

I would like to be less...
_____
_____
_____
_____
_____
_____
_____
_____
_____

I want to experience or do LESS of these things:
_____
_____
_____
_____
_____
_____
_____
_____
_____

What makes a good goal for change?

Just about everybody has things they would like to change in their lives. A particular change is more likely to happen when they make it a goal, a priority. Here are four things that make a good goal:

Your goal should be **ACHIEVABLE** – something that is possible and realistic. It doesn't have to be easy; it's okay for your goal to be challenging. Just make it doable.

Your goal should be **REWARDING** – something you really want that would make life better for you or others. When possible, state it as a positive change – something you want to increase, improve, create or strengthen.

Your goal should be **MEASURABLE** – a change that you and others can observe. How will you know you are making progress toward it?

Your goal should be **SPECIFIC** – General goals like, "I want to be a better person" aren't clear enough to work on. For a bigger long-term change project, one way to make a specific goal is to decide on the next step you want to take.

A
R
M
S

Make a goal something you can get your ARMS around.

Choosing your goals

Now look back over pages 4 through 7 and decide what are your three most important goals for change. Remember to make each goal one that you can get your ARMS around: make it Achievable, Rewarding, Measurable and Specific. Describe each of your ARMS goals below:

My first goal for change is: _____
_____
_____
_____
_____
_____

❏ Achievable
❏ Rewarding
❏ Measurable
❏ Specific

My second goal for change is: _____
_____
_____
_____
_____
_____

❏ Achievable
❏ Rewarding
❏ Measurable
❏ Specific

My third goal for change is: _____
_____
_____
_____
_____
_____

❏ Achievable
❏ Rewarding
❏ Measurable
❏ Specific

Your first goal

Here are some things to consider about your first goal. On the line below, write a short description of your first goal from page 8.

My first change goal is to: _____

Circle a number on the scale reflecting how *important* it is for you to make this change:

| 0 | 1 | 2 | 3 | 4 | 5 | 6 | 7 | 8 | 9 | 10 |

Not at all important   Extremely important

Why did you choose this number rather than a lower number or zero? Why is it important for you to make this change?

_____
_____
_____

Circle a number on the scale that reflects how *confident* you are about making this change:

| 0 | 1 | 2 | 3 | 4 | 5 | 6 | 7 | 8 | 9 | 10 |

I'm sure I can't   I'm sure I can

Why did you choose this number rather than a lower number or zero? What helps you believe that you can make this change?

_____
_____
_____

What do you need, or what would help you to succeed in making this change?

_____
_____
_____

It is illegal to duplicate this page in any manner.

Your second goal

My second change goal from page 8 is to: _____

_____

Circle a number on the scale reflecting how *important* it is for you to make this change:

0   1   2   3   4   5   6   7   8   9   10

Not at all important   Extremely important

Why did you choose this number rather than a lower number or zero? Why is it *important* for you to make this change?

_____
_____
_____
_____

Circle a number on the scale that reflects how *confident* you are about making this change:

0   1   2   3   4   5   6   7   8   9   10

I'm sure I can't   I'm sure I can

Why did you choose this number rather than a lower number or zero? What helps you believe that you can make this change?

_____
_____
_____
_____

What do you need, or what would help you to succeed in making this change?

_____
_____
_____
_____

Your third goal

My third change goal from page 8 is to: _____

_____

Circle a number on the scale reflecting how *important* it is for you to make this change:

0   1   2   3   4   5   6   7   8   9   10

Not at all important   Extremely important

Why did you choose this number rather than a lower number or zero? Why is it *important* for you to make this change?

_____
_____
_____
_____

Circle a number on the scale that reflects how *confident* you are about making this change:

0   1   2   3   4   5   6   7   8   9   10

I'm sure I can't   I'm sure I can

Why did you choose this number rather than a lower number or zero? What helps you believe that you can make this change?

_____
_____
_____
_____

What do you need, or what would help you to succeed in making this change?

_____
_____
_____
_____

Resources for change

Now it's time to think about what resources will support you in making the changes you choose. To begin with, think about your personal strengths that will help you succeed.

Below are some words that describe successful changers. Look through the list and put a check mark (✔) on at least five that you think particularly apply to you. Feel free to add your own to the list.

Characteristics of successful changers

☐ Accepting	☐ Clever	☐ Flexible	☐ Persistent
☐ Active	☐ Committed	☐ Focused	☐ Positive
☐ Adaptable	☐ Competent	☐ Forgiving	☐ Powerful
☐ Adventurous	☐ Concerned	☐ Forward-looking	☐ Quick
☐ Affectionate	☐ Confident	☐ Happy	☐ Reasonable
☐ Affirmative	☐ Considerate	☐ Healthy	☐ Receptive
☐ Alert	☐ Courageous	☐ Hopeful	☐ Relaxed
☐ Ambitious	☐ Creative	☐ Imaginative	☐ Reliable
☐ Anchored	☐ Decisive	☐ Intelligent	☐ Resourceful
☐ Assertive	☐ Dedicated	☐ Loving	☐ Responsible
☐ Assured	☐ Determined	☐ Mature	☐ Sensible
☐ Attentive	☐ Diligent	☐ Open	☐ Skillful
☐ Brave	☐ Eager	☐ Optimistic	☐ Solid
☐ Bright	☐ Earnest	☐ Orderly	☐ Stable
☐ Bold	☐ Effective	☐ Organized	☐ Steady
☐ Capable	☐ Energetic	☐ Patient	☐ Straight
☐ Careful	☐ Faithful	☐ Perceptive	☐ Strong
☐ Cheerful	☐ Fearless	☐ Persevering	☐ Thankful

In your own words

Choose the five characteristics that best describe you, and write them below. In what ways are you like this? Where in your life have you particularly shown this quality?

Characteristic #1: I am _____.
Tell how this describes you: I _____
_____
_____

- ☐ Thorough
- ☐ Tough
- ☐ Trusting
- ☐ Trustworthy
- ☐ Truthful
- ☐ Understanding
- ☐ Vigorous
- ☐ Visionary
- ☐ Whole
- ☐ Willing
- ☐ Winning
- ☐ Wise
- ☐ Worthy
- ☐ Zealous
- ☐ _____
- ☐ _____
- ☐ _____

Characteristic #2: I am _____.
Tell how this describes you: I _____
_____
_____

Characteristic #3: I am _____.
Tell how this describes you: I _____
_____
_____

Characteristic #4: I am _____.
Tell how this describes you: I _____
_____
_____

Characteristic #5: I am _____.
Tell how this describes you: I _____
_____
_____

Who can help?

Besides yourself, who might be able to help you make the changes you want in your life? These supporters might be family, friends, spiritual leaders, health professionals, teachers, co-workers or others you know. Who could help you and how might they help?

One person who might help me with the changes I want to make is: _____

This person could help me by: _____

_____

_____

_____

Someone else who might help me with the changes I want to make is: _____

This person could help me by: _____

_____

_____

_____

Someone else who might help me with the changes I want to make is: _____

This person could help me by: _____

_____

_____

_____

Recovery

What about your longer-term hopes? What future do you wish for yourself and those you love? Recovery is all about the positive changes you hope for, not only escaping from a current problem or illness. It is about returning to or finding a place of health and balance.

Think about what your life might be like in the future if you made mental balance a priority and no longer used alcohol or illicit drugs. What do you hope your life will be like with your:

Family: _____
_____
_____

Work or School: _____
_____
_____

Role in Your Community: _____
_____
_____

Finances: _____
_____
_____

Health: _____
_____
_____

Spirituality: _____
_____
_____

What are feelings?

Your feelings or emotions are personal to you. Although someone else may be able to guess how you are feeling by your appearance or from the things you say, only you know for sure what you are experiencing.

Some people find it quite easy to identify and name how they are feeling. Others find it more difficult or confusing, perhaps because it is possible to experience a mixture of different and unique feelings. Sometimes you'll even experience feelings that seem opposed to each other (for example, feeling sadness, anger and relief about the end of a relationship).

Feelings are also sometimes confused with thoughts. This is because thoughts and feelings are closely linked, as is discussed later in this Journal.

A simple test to see if something is a thought or a feeling is to use the word, "that." For example, a person might say, "I feel that I'm doing OK," or "I feel that you're disrespecting me." If the word "that" logically follows the word "feel," then it's not a feeling – it's a thought. Even if a person uses a phrase where "that" could be inserted, it's still a thought. "I feel I'm doing fine" and "I feel you are disrespecting me."

Another way to check if something is a thought or feeling is to see if the word "think" can be sensibly substituted for "feel": "I think I'm doing fine" and "I think you are disrespecting me." If so, it's probably a thought rather than a feeling.

On the other hand, when actual feelings are being described, it makes no sense to substitute the word, "think." "I feel sad" makes sense. "I think sad" just doesn't sound right.

Feelings from A to Z

Here are some of the many names for common feelings people often experience. Circle those feelings you experience most often. Feel free to add other emotions you often feel (that's what the extra lines at the end are for). Finally, cross out feelings you rarely experience.

Afraid	Frightened	Lonely	Stubborn
Angry	Frustrated	Lost	Tense
Annoyed	Furious	Loving	Uncomfortable
Anxious	Guilty	Miserable	Vengeful
Bitter	Happy	Nervous	Worried
Bored	Hateful	Outraged	Zany
Carefree	Hopeful	Overwhelmed	Zestful
Caring	Hopeless	Passionate	_____
Confused	Horrified	Peaceful	_____
Disappointed	Hurt	Pleased	_____
Disgusted	Hysterical	Rejected	_____
Down	Indifferent	Relieved	_____
Ecstatic	Interested	Resentful	_____
Embarrassed	Jealous	Sad	_____
Empty	Joyful	Sexy	_____
Envious	Kooky	Shocked	_____
Excited	Lazy	Shy	_____
Exhausted	Lighthearted	Sorry	_____

Self-understanding and the STORC Cycle

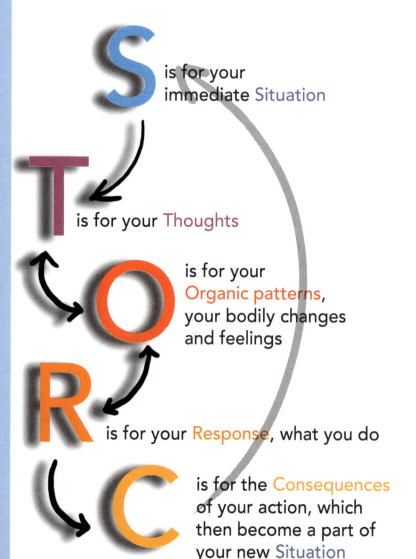

S is for your immediate Situation

T is for your Thoughts

O is for your Organic patterns, your bodily changes and feelings

R is for your Response, what you do

C is for the Consequences of your action, which then become a part of your new Situation

Your feelings and actions don't just happen randomly. So where do they come from? Would you believe the STORC brings them?

STORC is a sequence of five events. When you feel stuck, it's often the same STORC pattern repeating over and over, like a broken record. The good news is that it's usually possible to change several of the components of STORC, and changing any one of them affects the others and can change the whole pattern.

> You have a lot of say about what happens to you, as well as how you feel and think.

Situations

S

Let's take the pieces of the STORC cycle one at a time.

The S in STORC stands for the Situation in which you find yourself at any given moment. It's whatever is happening around you. This would include:

- The time of day or night
- The people around you and what they are doing or saying
- The temperature, surroundings, noise level
- Everything outside your skin that your senses can detect

There is a temptation to blame your feelings and experiences on the Situation around you:

- I yelled at them because they were noisy
- The food smelled good and that's why I ate it
- She made me sad (mad, happy, scared)
- I cheated because I was pressured to win

Can you think of times when you blamed your feelings or reactions on the outside Situation? What are some examples?

_____
_____
_____
_____
_____
_____
_____
_____

> It's true that people react to their Situations, but how you respond is rarely automatic. With STORC, you have plenty of chances to make a healthy choice.

Thought patterns

T

The T in STORC stands for how you Think about your Situation – how you recognize and make sense of it. Just as you usually have some choice about the Situation you're in, you also can choose how you think about it, and it does matter what you Think.

Consider something as potentially important in your Situation as a dog barking at you. How you feel and what you do will have a lot to do with how you Think about your Situation. It will depend on:

- How well you know the dog (if at all)
- What you think about its breed (wiener dog, pit bull, German shepherd)
- Whether you believe the barking is friendly or aggressive
- Whether you think it can get to you

Thinking the wrong thing about a Situation could have disastrous consequences, especially if your response is based on that misunderstanding.

Describe a time when misunderstanding a situation got you in trouble.

_____
_____
_____
_____
_____

Organic patterns

The O in STORC stands for your Organic patterns, meaning your body. These patterns have to do with physical changes that happen inside of you. Sweating, shivering, tightening of muscles, changes in your body chemistry and emotions are all examples of these changes. Just thinking about something can affect your body. This is called the mind-body connection.

Imagine slicing open and biting into one of these sour lemons. Can you feel the glands under your tongue making saliva?

That's the mind-body connection at work.

Thoughts and feelings are not completely separate. Thinking about times when you felt happy or sad, confused or angry, tends to bring back those same feelings. Some feelings, like frustration, are brought on by thinking about your Situation.

People whose sympathetic nervous system starts pumping for some reason (heart rate and blood pressure increase, breathing faster) will feel differently depending on whether they interpret it as anger, fear, elation or being "psyched."

Some body reactions are automatic and happen even before you can think about them, such as when you're startled by a sudden unexpected loud noise, or your knee jerking when a doctor taps it with a rubber reflex hammer.

Many body reactions, however, are learned and can be relearned. Some body changes result directly from what you do: relaxing, meditating and exercising. Medications, alcohol and other psychoactive drugs also produce changes in your organic patterns.

"So *that's* why they're called knee-jerk reactions."

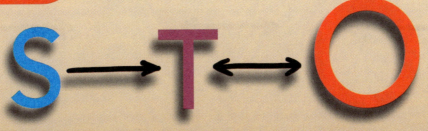

Responses

R The R in STORC stands for how you Respond to your Situation, Thoughts and Organic patterns. Your Response is what you do; your behavior or actions. Behaviors are learned (and relearned), but you also choose them.

We hold people responsible for what they do because they could have chosen to do otherwise. "He made me do it," is not usually a good defense in court. In almost any Situation, you have a choice about how to Think and feel about it and how you Respond.

"I'm usually so burned out after work that I can't do anything. I just lie on my bed and worry. Getting high is the only thing that makes me feel better."

"I thought I was okay to drive. And I thought I was doing pretty good. I had myself convinced I was sober until the officer asked me to walk a straight line."

"When he was late getting home, I thought he was still at work. But I called the office and he wasn't there, and I couldn't reach him on his cell. After two hours I called the police."

S → T ↔ O ↔ R

Consequences

Finally, C is for Consequences – how your Situation changes as a result of your actions. This includes how others react to your behavior. It also includes physical changes in the world around you: broken glass, a new fence or the balance in your bank account. Consequences are the direct or indirect result of your responses. Sometimes negative consequences can be prevented or changed by prior protective actions such as wearing a seat belt or buying insurance.

What protective actions have you taken to prevent negative consequences for you or your loved ones? What actions do you plan to take?

___

S → T ↔ O ↔ R ↔ C

Self-management

Some aspects of your Situation, Organic patterns and Consequences are beyond your control and not a matter of choice. It's just how things are. Think about your body as an example. Your body is partly a product of the genes you inherited from your parents as well as your environment and lifestyle. You can't change where you came from, but you can guide yourself toward where you'd like to go.

It is wise advice:

- To accept the things we cannot change
- To change the things we can
- To seek the wisdom to know the difference

Many people underestimate how much they can change and manage the course of their lives. Recognize that you're in control of your destiny and use that knowledge to help your effort along.

That is what self-management is all about.

"Self-control is not something you *have*, it's something you *do*."

STORC analysis

STORC is a tool for understanding yourself – your Thoughts, Organic patterns and Responses and their relationship with your Situation. Remember the A-B-C cycle on page 4? Cognition, Affect and Behavior correspond to the Thinking, Organic patterns and Response elements of STORC. They are the ones that arise inside your skin and are closely tied together. They are also where you can make the most choices to practice self-control and self-determination.

To get a better idea of how the STORC cycle works, let's apply it to four different experiences: anger, stress, urges and cravings and substance use. Which of these four experiences influences you the most in your day-to-day life? Why?

_____
_____
_____
_____
_____
_____
_____
_____
_____
_____

You
Anger
Stress
Urges and Cravings
Substance Use

Anger

The experience of anger is a good place to start in understanding STORC because the steps are often fairly clear. It is easiest to think of the first step, the Situations that "make you mad." Some common Situations might be feeling hurt or being in pain, being surprised or startled, being criticized or challenged or not getting something you want.

Think of three recent Situations where you felt angry. On page 27, briefly describe three Situations that "made you mad."

Now fill in the Thought column. Do you remember what you were thinking about this Situation – what you said to yourself? If you're not sure, what must you have said to yourself that led to feeling that way in this Situation?

Next fill in the middle (Organic patterns) column describing how you felt. Do you remember any feelings or changes in your body? What were your emotions?

Next fill in the Response column. What did you do in response to your angry feeling?

Finally fill in the Consequence column. What happened as a result of your action?

"Sometimes when I get real mad it's like someone else takes over, someone I don't even recognize. I really need to work on fixing my anger problem."

Analyzing anger

Situation What was happening?	Thought What did you think to yourself?	Organic patterns What did you feel?	Response What did you do?	Consequence What happened next as a result?
Example My girlfriend didn't show up for dinner at my place as planned.	How could she? She didn't even call to let me know. She must be with someone else.	Annoyed. Tight stomach. Then furious. Lonely.	Drank. Turned on the TV. Smashed a picture. Cried some. Left an angry message on her voice mail.	Fell asleep on the couch. She apologized for forgetting. We aren't talking now.
Situation 1				
Situation 2				
Situation 3				

Stress

A second kind of feeling that is useful to analyze with the STORC cycle is stress – feeling anxious, nervous, upset or stressed out. Think of three **Situations** where this has happened to you. On page 29, describe them in the **Situations** column.

Now fill in the **Thought** column. Do you remember what you were thinking about this **Situation** – what you said to yourself? If you're not sure, what must you have said to yourself in order to feel the way you did about this **Situation**?

Next fill in the middle (**Organic patterns**) column describing how you felt. Do you remember any feelings or changes in your body? What were your emotions?

Next fill in the **Response** column. What did you do in response to your feelings?

Finally fill in the **Consequence** column. What happened as a result of your action?

> "When I got laid off from my job, I was stressed and scared. Then I realized my situation might be a blessing in disguise. This is my chance to make the career switch I have been wanting."

Think of a time you were stressed to your limit. How do you plan to avoid that level of stress in the future?

Analyzing stress

Situation What was happening?	Thought What did you think to yourself?	Organic Patterns What did you feel?	Response What did you do?	Consequence What happened next as a result?
Example My car broke down again; just quit running at a stop light.	Not again! What am I going to do? I can't afford to buy a car. I don't know what to do.	Embarrassed. Hopeless. Tight in my chest. Frustrated.	Called a friend to push me to the gas station.	Paid $80 to get the car running again.
Situation 1				
Situation 2				
Situation 3				

Urges and craving

Urges or "craving" to drink or use also can be understood using the STORC cycle. Here we'll take a slightly different approach.

On the opposite page, in the Triggers column, list some of the circumstances in which you might feel like using your usual drug(s). These can be situations, things you are thinking, feeling or doing.

Now fill in the boxes in the column that says: "What I hope will happen if I drink or use drugs."

Finally, consider what else you might do instead of using alcohol or other drugs to get the same or better results. (If you can't think of anything else you could do, that's a form of psychological dependence on a chemical. It's the only way you know to get the effect you want.)

The examples below can help you complete your own chart on page 31.

Triggers	What I hope will happen if I drink or use drugs	Alternatives
Situations • At a party with friends • Alone at home after work • Just got a failing grade at school	• Join in - have fun • Relax and get high • Take the edge off frustration	
Thoughts • Thinking about my past • Feeling sorry for myself • Hopeless	• Forget • Shut down • Don't think about it	
Feelings • Thirsty • Frustrated or angry • Feeling down or nervous • Feeling sick	• Quench thirst • Lighten up • Feel better • Feel better	
Actions • Having sex • Watching TV • Dancing	• Better sex • Pass the time • Relax, feel comfortable	

Analyzing urges and craving

Triggers	What I hope will happen if I drink or use drugs	Alternatives
Situations		
Thoughts		
Feelings		
Actions		

Substance use

Finally, the STORC cycle can be used to understand Situations in which you return to drinking or using drugs after a period of nonuse, even though you did not want or intend to.

Think of a situation in which you did not intend to drink or use, but wound up doing so (or drinking or using more than you intended). Use the STORC cycle to think about what happened.

This same method can be used to understand other situations in which you slipped back to an older way of behaving, one that you had intended to leave behind. This is actually fairly common: think about New Year's resolutions. Imperfection is a part of human nature.

On page 33, fill in the STORC chart for Situations in which this happened to you. The Response here would be the behavior you had wanted to avoid (such as drinking or using). What was the Situation that led up to this? What were you Thinking and what were your Organic patterns telling you just before it happened? What were the Consequences?

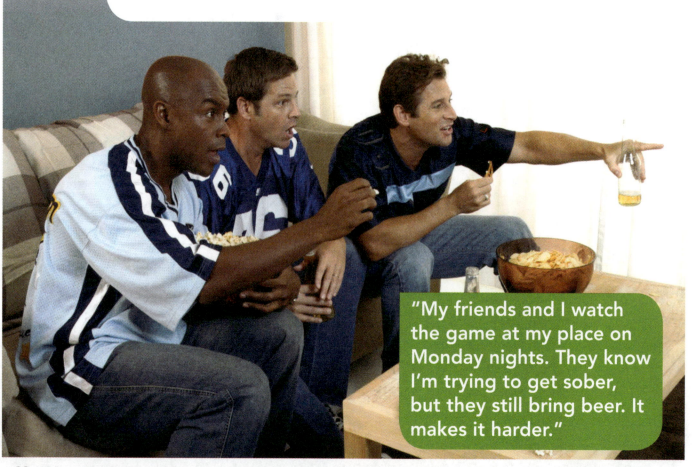

"My friends and I watch the game at my place on Monday nights. They know I'm trying to get sober, but they still bring beer. It makes it harder."

Analyzing substance use

Situation What was happening?	Thought What did you think to yourself?	Organic Patterns What did you feel?	Response What did you do?	Consequence What happened next as a result?
Example My cousin's wedding with an open bar.	I'll just have one or two drinks. It can't hurt. Besides, it's free!	Excited, a little guilty.	Had a lot of drinks.	Stayed until the bar closed. Don't remember all that I did.
Situation 1				
Situation 2				
Situation 3				

Using the STORC for change

> As you work through this section of the Journal, it will be helpful for you to look back at the goals you set for yourself on pages 9-11. You will be applying what you learn about STORC to reach your goals.

At each step in the STORC cycle there are usually a number of different things you can do to promote change. For any of the change goals you identified earlier, you may be able to come up with a dozen or more possible things you can do to make a difference. It is possible that you'll find one that makes a big difference, but more often what happens is that each little change makes some difference, and it is the combined effect of several smaller changes that moves you toward where you want to go.

Think of this as experimenting with your own psychology. The STORC model can help you think of many different possible ways to move toward change. Try them out, perhaps one at a time, and give them some time to work. See which ones result in a noticeable improvement for you. One size does not fit all, and even mental health professionals are not particularly good at guessing which approaches will help you the first time. The point is to keep trying things until you find what works for you.

> **Look back at your first goal on page 9. How many different things can you think of that might help you move toward this goal? Brainstorm some of them below.**
>
> _____
> _____
> _____
> _____
> _____
> _____
> _____
> _____
>
> **If you can't think of many options yet, keep reading. The rest of this Journal is designed to help you think of different possibilities.**

Change your Situation

S

The first link in the STORC chain is S, the Situation in which you find yourself. These are things outside your skin, but nevertheless you often have a lot of choice about them. There are many things you can change about your situation.

Many of the examples used in this Journal are about alcohol/drug use and problems because that is what just about everyone who uses this Journal has in common. However, the very same brainstorming approach can be used at each step in the STORC cycle to come up with ways to make changes in other areas of your life as well.

To help you get an idea how to use STORC in this way, pick out one of the three change goals you described on pages 9-11. Which one of the three seems highest priority for you right now? As you go through the pages that follow and the steps of the STORC cycle, be thinking about your own change goal and how the information applies to it.

> Remember the three goals you set on pages 9-11. You can use STORC to achieve them.

S
T
O
R
C

Which one of your change goals will you use for practice, and why?

_____
_____
_____
_____
_____
_____
_____

Identify
problem Situations

One way to take charge is to identify those Situations that are most likely to lead in the wrong direction. These are sometimes called:

- **Slippery places**
- **Trouble spots**
- **High-risk situations**
- **Triggers**

In what external Situations are you most likely to experience problems, urges or temptations, stress, feeling low or whatever it is that you want to change? Where are your slippery places regarding your change goal?

Places _____

_____

_____

People _____

_____

_____

Activities _____

_____

_____

Things you see or hear _____

_____

_____

Times of the day/week _____

_____

_____

Keep track

Often people are not aware of all the Situational factors that set off problems for them. One way to find out is to keep a record for a week or two. If you are tracking urges to drink or use, notice when your urges are weaker or stronger, and also when they are not there. You might use a scale from 1 to 10 for how strong your urge or temptation feels, and also keep a record of anything that might be related: time and day, where you are, whom you are with, what you are doing, etc.

Similarly, if you're tracking your mood, you could use a rating scale from 1 (feeling really bad) to 10 (feeling really good). Maybe what you decide to track is a particular behavior, like having a drink or saying something critical or nice to other people. It's up to you exactly what you want to track. Be a detective about your own life! Find out what Situational factors seem to be linked with the problems you want to change, and also with doing or feeling better.

S^2

T
O
R
C

What could you keep a record of in your diary? _____

How would you measure it? _____

What are your best guesses about Situational factors you should keep track of that may be related to what you're measuring?

Avoid slippery places

In English class you may have learned that nouns are words for people, places or things. Once you identify (or maybe you already know) the Situational factors that are likely to cause trouble for you, one possible option is to avoid those particular people, places or things. Of course it's not always possible to avoid all such Situations, but consider what you can avoid! Especially in the early stages of change, it's wise to avoid trouble spots and triggers as best you can.

S³

T
O
R
C

Some possible examples of avoiding are:

- Removing reminders of temptation from your home
- Staying away from certain people
- Keeping out of certain places
- Not doing specific things that are particularly risky

Avoiding is only one of dozens of possible strategies explored in this Journal, so don't worry if it seems like avoidance won't solve all your problems. It won't, but it's one good option.

What Situational factors could you avoid in the weeks ahead to help you make the changes you want?

_____
_____
_____
_____
_____
_____
_____
_____

Take along insurance

It's rarely possible to avoid all higher-risk Situations, and so some planning ahead can be helpful for when you do find yourself in a slippery spot. If you know in advance that you're going to be in a riskier Situation, what "insurance" could you take along or plan ahead to help you get through it? There are lots of options such as:

- Taking along a supportive friend or family member
- Having an escape plan (like taking a taxi)
- Carrying a reminder in your pocket (like AA coins)
- Taking along little or no money
- Asking a friend to pick you up at a certain time
- Plan an activity afterward that starts at a set time (like a show)

S^4

T O R C

Think about Situations where making or maintaining your change may be more challenging. What "insurance" could you take with you into such Situations?

_____
_____
_____
_____
_____
_____
_____
_____

Change your environment

It is also possible to make small modifications in your own environment to support and encourage the changes you want to make. Here are a few examples:

Reminders. When you're trying to do something new, it often helps to have little prompts to remind you to be conscious about what you do. The time-conscious person might place a small colored dot on the face of a wristwatch, using this as a reminder to relax and slow down. A colored sticker on your speedometer can similarly serve as a reminder to slow down. Many people place a note or picture on their refrigerator door, prompting them to ask, "Do I really need to eat now?" A small alarm on a watch or cell phone can serve as a reminder to take a medication or to pause and take a few deep breaths.

Purchases. Sometimes simple purchases can facilitate change. Exercising might be helped along by buying a good pair of running shoes and a warm-up suit. Roommates with different tastes in music may decrease conflicts just by purchasing headphones. The stress of parenting small children can be reduced by childproofing the house, placing breakables out of reach, putting locks on cabinets and drawers with hazardous materials and installing a gate across the entrance to a steep set of stairs.

Rearranging. It is also helpful at times to rearrange what you already have. Some people symbolize a change they are making by rearranging furniture or by moving to a different apartment. Relaxing can be facilitated by arranging a comfortable chair in a quiet and distraction-free room.

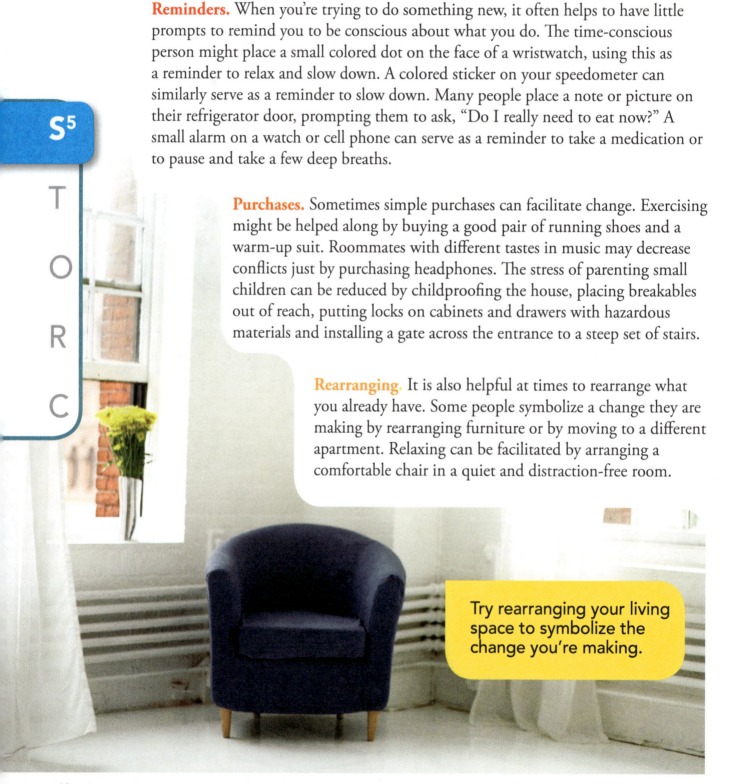

Try rearranging your living space to symbolize the change you're making.

Ask others for help

Sometimes other people can help change your Situation too. Ask them to help you make the changes you want. Let them know what you are wanting to change and how they can help.

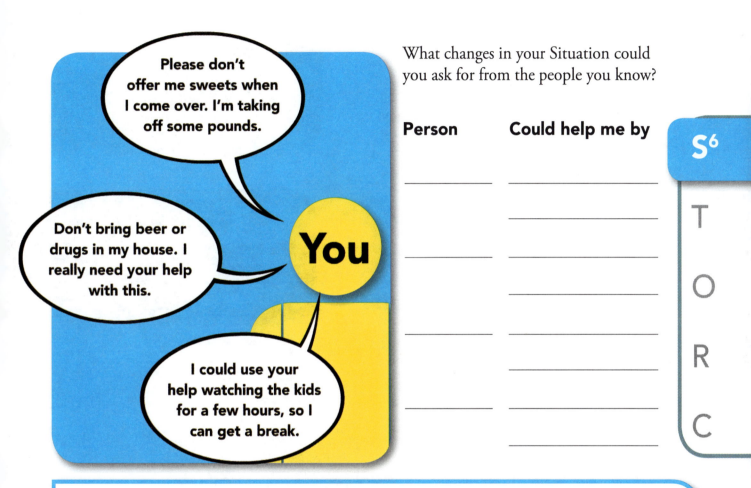

What changes in your Situation could you ask for from the people you know?

Person	Could help me by
_____	_____
_____	_____
_____	_____
_____	_____
_____	_____
_____	_____

S⁶ TORC

Pick one of the people you have mentioned above and think through exactly how you might ask him or her to make this change to help you. You might start your sentence with, "I would really appreciate it if you would…," or "You could really help me by…"

_____
_____
_____
_____
_____

Surround yourself...

Even if you really want to change some thought, feeling or behavior, it can still be hard especially if you try to do that all by yourself. If you're fortunate enough to already be surrounded by people who support your recovery, good for you! But, if support for change is not all around you, then consider going where you can find a whole ready-made community of people rooting for you. Recovery support groups are self-help groups where people are working together on change. They are mostly mutual-help groups where people help each other and in the process help themselves as well.

In many communities there are all kinds of mutual-help groups. You might have to try several before you find where you are most comfortable and where you are getting the best support. Here are some that might be available close to where you live and open to you several times a week. If not, chances are there is at least one of these groups in your area.

First, there are the Twelve-Step programs.

Alcoholics Anonymous (AA) – For people who have a desire to quit drinking. Even if you are not sure, you are welcome to listen and learn from the experiences of others. www.aa.org

Narcotics Anonymous (NA) – For people who have a desire to quit drugs other than alcohol. There are also more specific groups like Cocaine Anonymous. www.na.org

Dual Recovery Anonymous (DRA) and Dual Diagnosis Anonymous (DDA) – For people recovering from mental health and substance use problems. www.draonline.org

...with **support**

There are lots of other similar groups that are based on the same philosophy of the Twelve Steps and Twelve Traditions such as Methadone Anonymous (MA); Gamblers Anonymous (GA); Overeaters Anonymous (OA); Sex and Love Addicts Anonymous (SLAA); and Schizophrenia Anonymous (SA).

Family members and any person affected by someone else's addiction can attend Al-Anon, or Nar-Anon, which is more specifically for families of those with drug problems. There are even groups for young people whose lives have been affected by someone else's drinking or drug use, called Alateen. Double Trouble in Recovery (DTR) was designed to meet the needs of people who have addictive substance problems as well as having been diagnosed with a psychiatric disorder.

There are also support groups for people that are not based on a Twelve-Step approach.

Which group might be best for you?

Moderation Management is a national recovery program and support group network for people who have decided to reduce their drinking.
www.moderation.org

Secular Organizations for Sobriety (SOS) is an alternative recovery method for those alcoholics or drug addicts who are uncomfortable with the spiritual content of 12-Step programs.
www.cfiwest.org/sos/index.htm

SMART Recovery offers free support groups to individuals who desire to gain independence from any type of addictive behavior.
www.smartrecovery.org

Women For Sobriety (WFS) is dedicated to helping women overcome alcohol and other drug problems.
www.womenforsobriety.org

Where to start

With so many options, it can be tough figuring out where to start. Here are some questions to help you consider which group might be a good fit for you.

> 1. Have you ever found a support group that helped you, even if just for a short time? That might be the group to try again as a place to start.
>
> 2. Do you know anyone who attends a support group and finds it helpful? Ask to go along to a meeting to see what you think.
>
> 3. Have you heard something about a particular support group that sparks some interest for you? Look them up on the Internet or ask someone about them. Try a meeting.

It's probably easier to attend an established support group than to create your own. But some people would rather use their church or spiritual community or some other group they already belong to. Just be sure there are enough people who understand what you are going through to be there for you when you need them. You have a higher chance of being with people who really understand you when you attend one of the established support groups.

If no organized mutual-help groups appeal to you, create the same kind of helpful features that work in support groups: a coach, mentor or successful person in recovery who can guide you in your recovery; a group of people who understand what you are going through and accept you just as you are, whatever level of growth you are at; people who won't mind if you need to call any time day or night to get their advice or help; a social group who you can hang out with during holidays or community events that may be stressful for you to be alone (for example, New Year's Eve or St. Patrick's Day).

What are your own thoughts at this point about a mutual-help or support group that might work for you? What group(s) might you like to check out?

_____

_____

_____

_____

_____

Who else?

Who else might be able to give you help and support on your road to recovery? These should, of course, be people who would definitely not tempt or encourage you to drink or use. Think of people who themselves have healthy, drug-free lives, and who might be willing to help and support you in your recovery. How about:

People in my family or extended family:
_____
_____

Friends, co-workers or other healthy peers:
_____
_____

Professional helpers (counselor, therapist, physician, etc.):
_____
_____

Religious professionals:
_____
_____

Teachers, mentors or role models:
_____
_____

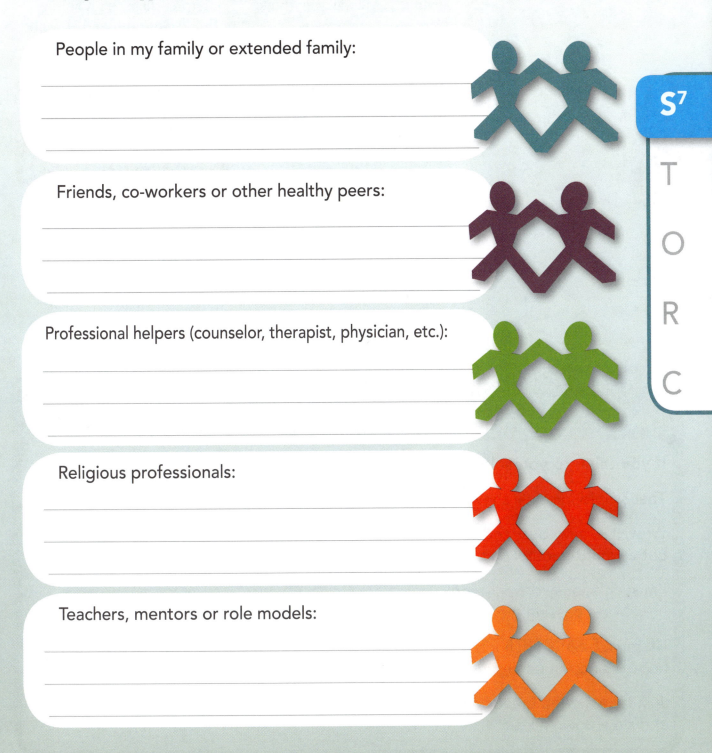

Change your Thinking

The second link in the STORC chain is T, the way you Think. Here is something you definitely have a choice about. You get to choose how you will think about things, what your attitude will be. That choice is, in fact, something no one can ever take away from you.

It is common for people to say things like, "You made me mad," or "The news story made me feel scared." But, consider this idea: there is nothing – no Situation – that automatically makes you feel a certain way. It's not clear how Situations will influence you until you interpret them. It's how you Think about things that really drives how you feel.

> What do you think about the idea that nothing can automatically make you have certain feelings?

If this is true, that it's your interpretation of what happens that most affects how you feel and respond, then how you think really matters! It makes a difference what you say to yourself.

Imagine that you're driving on a busy street and another car cuts into the lane right in front of you so that you have to slow down. How would you be likely to feel if you said these different things to yourself?

If you think to yourself:

That stupid idiot! I'll show him!

Wow, it's really busy today, but a what beautiful day!

I'm such a lousy driver, people are always passing me.

He must be in a big hurry – hope it's not an emergency.

Just take a deep breath, relax and slow down a little.

You might feel:

_____

_____

_____

_____

_____

Become aware of troubling thoughts

You may be well aware of thoughts that trouble you, but sometimes it also takes a little detective work. Sometimes these thoughts happen so quickly and automatically that you may not be conscious of them. It may be possible to reason backward, to ask yourself, "If this is what I was feeling, then I must have been saying this to myself to make me feel that way." Think of some situations in which you have felt each of these ways, and consider what you might have been thinking to get you there.

Feelings	What might I have said to myself that made me feel this way?
Angry, Annoyed, Frustrated, Furious	
Anxious, Nervous, Worried, Frightened	
Stressed out, Tense, Pressured	
Down, Hurt, Sad, Discouraged	

S

T¹

O

R

C

You can also keep a feelings diary like the one below, for a week or so, to discover self-talk that may be troubling you. When you experience a significant negative feeling, describe it in the Feeling column. Then make a note of the Situation in which you felt this way. Finally, fill in the middle Thought column. What *must* you have said to yourself to get from this Situation to your Feeling?

The Situation	My Thoughts	My Feeling

Stop your thoughts

S
T²
O
R
C

Just because a thought comes into your head does not mean you have to keep it playing. Some thoughts are fuel for negative emotions. Anger, for example, is like fire. It needs fairly constant new fuel and air to keep burning. Take away the fuel or the oxygen and it quickly dies. Resentful thoughts are particularly flammable. Resentment involves blaming someone for part of your current situation. The more you think bitter and resentful thoughts, the angrier you are likely to feel. Anxiety works in much the same way, only it is fueled by worry. If you keep fretting about unpleasant things that might happen, you are likely to feel the flame of fear in your belly.

I'm late for work because that guy cut me off **STOP** *but I probably could have left earlier.*

One simple tool you can try is called thought-stopping. When you catch yourself thinking thoughts that cause you trouble, stop it! Don't continue following these thoughts that lead you in the wrong direction. Thought-stopping is about turning off the fuel.

Take one of the themes you identified on the previous page as causing you distress. Begin rehearsing those familiar lines to yourself, and once you get going, shout out loud, "Stop it!" (You might want to be alone when you try this!) The act of saying, "Stop it" interrupts the thought process. Fortunately, you don't have to keep on shouting this out loud. Turn down the volume to normal speaking, then whispering, and eventually you can just think to yourself, "Stop it!" The point is to interrupt your troubling thought process rather than allowing it to continue running.

> **Sometimes it helps to have a "bridge phrase" to get the reevaluation started:**
> - Now wait just a minute…
> - Hold on now…
> - I know better than that…

Reevaluate

Stopping your troubling thoughts is a good start, but what next? Another good tool is to come up with "antidote" thoughts, like the antidote to a poison. This is essentially a reevaluation that gives you new self-talk to replace the old talk. The basic pattern goes like this:

OLD TALK → **STOP** → **NEW TALK**

This means coming up with new talk to replace the old. It may be helpful here to consider examples of common thinking errors that can lead to trouble.

Exaggeration

Exaggeration statements might begin, "He always..." or "I will never be able to..." Exaggeration talk includes "catastrophizing": telling yourself how "awful" or "terrible" or "completely unfair" your situation is. It also can take something that is temporary and make it sound permanent.

Pessimism

Pessimistic statements focus only on the negative, bad or discouraging parts of a situation. However, reality is seldom black and white. Use optimism instead. Look for the good in others, find hope in a tough situation. Try to catch your kids doing something good. Pessimism leads to negative emotions.

Think about a recent situation where you used an exaggeration or pessimistic statement. How might you have thought about the situation in a positive way?

_____
_____
_____
_____
_____

Change your self-talk

In the "Old Self-Talk" boxes below, write down some of the things you have said to yourself that have leaned you toward negative feelings and trouble. Then in the "New Self-Talk" boxes write what you might say to yourself instead to reevaluate your situation in a more positive direction.

OLD SELF-TALK	NEW SELF-TALK
Oh, just one or two drinks can't hurt!	Now wait a minute! Yes they can! Remember what happened the last time I thought I'd have just a few? I don't want to do that again.

Think positive

When you want to have a good relationship with someone, it's good to remember to say positive things: to voice your appreciation for who the person is, and what she or he does. This often happens at the beginning of a relationship, but over time it can decrease (which is called "taking for granted") unless you intentionally remember to keep it up. The balance of positive and negative comments to each other is a pretty good indicator of the current quality and happiness of a relationship.

The same is true of your relationship with yourself. If you are constantly running yourself down, you're bound to feel down. On the other hand, if you remind yourself of your own good qualities and celebrate the positive things you do, it tends to give you a lift. It's a bit like taking vitamins every day. Of course it's also nice if you have supportive friends who remind you of your good qualities as well.

> To make sure that you are not overly focused on the negative, also talk to yourself about what is *right* with you.

Below, write six positive (and true) statements about yourself. For some hints on what to write, look back over pages 12 and 13 where you identified some of your strengths.

1. _____
2. _____
3. _____
4. _____
5. _____
6. _____

Try mental **rehearsal**

Suppose you were a professional athlete. Do you think it would make a difference if you simply imagined over and over making all the right moves, doing everything right to achieve peak performance? Turns out it does make a difference, and some athletes hire professional sports psychologists to help them do exactly that.

You can be your own coach. When there is a change you would like to make, run through in your thoughts how you could do it successfully. Practice your new thoughts and behaviors mentally. Imagine doing it easily and well, without discomfort.

What change would you like to make where rehearsing it mentally might be helpful? Describe in words, step by step, how you would succeed in making this change:

_____
_____
_____
_____
_____
_____
_____
_____
_____
_____
_____
_____
_____
_____

Coach yourself

By now you should be getting the idea that talking to yourself is not a problem, but rather a skill. With mental rehearsal you can practice in advance what you want to do well. But it is also possible to take your "coach" with you in real life.

Imagine that you are learning to ski, and have been in a class with an expert who has told you what you need to do. As you later head down the beginner slope, you can tell yourself what to do. "Bend your knees! Use your edges. Lean into the turn."

You can do the very same in situations where you want to strengthen your coping skills. Take your inner coach with you. If you're trying to strengthen your social skills, you might tell yourself: "Keep good eye contact and smile. Ask about the other person – most people love to talk about themselves. Relax and get to know this person!"

Think of a situation where you want to strengthen your skills. What things could you say to yourself, acting as your own coach?

Change your organic patterns

The third link in the STORC chain is O, your organic patterns, meaning your bodily changes and feelings. When you are in a particular Situation, and you have Thought about it – perceived and interpreted it – what is your body doing? You might think of this as something beyond your control, but actually you have a lot of choice about how you respond physically.

Relaxation

You might think of relaxation as doing nothing – "kicking back"– but it is also doing something – a skill. There are two particularly good ways of learning this skill, one more physical and the other more mental. Most people find that one of these works better for them than the other, so try them both.

Physical Relaxation

In the muscles of your body, the opposite of relaxation is tension. Relaxing has to do with letting go of the tension in your muscles. This has a way of calming your whole body. It takes some practice to learn how to release the tension in your muscles. Here's a way you can practice.

Find a quiet place to sit down in a comfortable recliner chair or lie on a rug. Working with one muscle group at a time, you will first tense the muscles for about five seconds, and then relax the muscle group, paying attention to the difference in how the muscles feel when tense and when relaxed. Do this twice for each muscle group, but never in a way that causes you pain. This works best with your eyes closed, so that you can really feel and focus on how the muscles feel when relaxing. Try it with the fifteen muscle groups on the next page:

54 • © 2010 The Change Companies®   It is illegal to duplicate this page in any manner.

Physical relaxation **exercises**

1. **Hands.** Squeeze your right hand into a fist, feel the tension, and then relax it. Repeat with the right hand, and then do it twice with your left hand.

2. **Forearms.** With your right arm lying straight and your palm facing down, bend at the wrist, pointing your fingers up and study the tension this creates. Release and repeat. Then do the same thing with your left hand and arm.

3. **Biceps.** Flex your upper arm muscles by touching your right shoulder with your right hand, tightening the biceps. Repeat on the right, then twice with the left arm.

4. **Shoulders.** Raise your shoulders up, as if to touch your ears with them. Release, relax, repeat.

5. **Forehead.** Raise your eyebrows up as far as they will go, wrinkling up your forehead. Release, relax, repeat.

6. **Face.** Squeeze your eyes tightly closed and wrinkle up your nose. Release, relax, repeat.

7. **Lips.** Press your lips together tightly. Release, relax, repeat.

8. **Tongue.** Push the tip of your tongue up into the roof of your mouth. Release, relax, repeat.

9. **Neck.** Press your head back against the chair or floor. Release, relax, repeat.

10. **Chest.** Take a deep breath and feel it stretch your chest muscles. Hold it, and then release it slowly, relaxing as you exhale. Repeat.

11. **Stomach.** Tighten up your stomach muscles, as though preparing to receive a punch. Release, relax, repeat.

12. **Back.** Arch your back away from the chair or floor. Release, relax, repeat.

13. **Legs and thighs.** Lift your legs up from the chair or floor, holding them straight out. Release, relax, repeat.

14. **Calves.** Tense your lower legs by flexing your toes toward your chest. Release, relax, repeat.

15. **Feet.** Curl your toes downward, as if digging them into warm sand. Release, relax, repeat.

Mental relaxation techniques

The "relaxation response" is a naturally occurring altered state of consciousness you can induce through the practice of a relatively simple method. The four essential parts of this method are:

- **Find a quiet place.** Get away from as many sources of noise and distraction as possible.

- **Find a comfortable position.** Choose one that minimizes muscle tension and that you can maintain for at least 20 minutes without moving.

- **Choose something to focus your attention on.** With eyes open, you could focus your gaze on a particular spot – a candle, any object or a blank wall. With eyes closed, you could focus on your slow and natural breathing.

- **Adopt a passive attitude.** This is the most important part of the relaxation response. If thoughts, memories or feelings drift into your awareness, just let them pass by like clouds. Don't hold onto them, but also don't try to keep them out. Keep bringing your attention back to your breathing or whatever you are focusing on.

Describe which of these relaxation techniques seems to work best for you.

_____
_____
_____
_____
_____

Eat **healthy**

It also makes a big difference what fuel you put into your body. Like exercise, eating healthy can help you maintain your mood, energy and weight, and prevent or manage chronic problems like heart disease, high blood pressure or diabetes. While your doctor or a dietician can give you specific advice about healthy eating, the five basic principles are fairly simple:

1. Eat more fresh vegetables and fruit – at least five servings a day.
2. Get enough protein. This doesn't have to be meat. Beans, nuts, fish and eggs are good sources of protein.
3. Eat more fiber.
4. Eat less fat and salt, and particularly high-fat high-salt fast foods.
5. Cut down on carbohydrates, especially white foods like sugar, white flour, pasta, potatoes and pretzels.

But, I don't like these foods!

Here's a little secret: We not only eat what we like, we like what we eat. Especially when you're hungry, satisfy your hunger with healthier food and your body will start liking it. Avoid junk food and fast food as a quick fix when you're hungry.

And experiment! There are far more kinds of vegetables, fruits and fibers than most people know. Try new foods and recipes. Widen the range of things you like.

What particular foods do you think you should eat less of?
_____
_____
_____

What particular healthy foods might you be able to eat more of instead?
_____
_____
_____

Some healthy foods

Circle foods below that you already enjoy. Then, underline more you could try, or could eat more often.

Almonds	Cabbage	Fava Beans
Apples	Cannellini beans	Figs
Apricots	Cantaloupe	Garbanzo beans
Artichokes	Carrots	Grapefruit
Asparagus	Cashews	Grapes
Avocado	Cauliflower	Green beans
Bananas	Celery	Guava
Barley	Cherries	Haricot beans
Bean sprouts	Chestnuts	Hazelnuts
Beets	Coconut	Hominy
Black beans	Corn	Jicama
Blackberries	Couscous	Kidney beans
Black-eyed peas	Cranberries	Kiwi
Blueberries	Cucumbers	Kumquats
Boysenberries	Currants	Lentils
Brocciflower	Dandelion greens	Lettuce
Broccoli	Dates	Lima beans
Brussels sprouts	Eggplant	Leeks
Bulgar	Escarole	Lychee nuts

Mango	Pinto beans	Sunflower seeds
Melons	Plums	Sweet potato
Mushrooms	Pomegranates	Swiss chard
Nectarines	Prunes	Tangerines
Oatmeal	Pumpkin	Tapioca
Okra	Pumpkinseeds	Tofu
Olives	Quinoa	Tomatoes
Onions	Quinces	Turnips
Oranges	Raisins	Walnuts
Papaya	Raspberries	Water chestnuts
Parsnips	Rhubarb	Watermelon
Peaches	Rice	Wax beans
Peanuts	Snap peas	White beans
Pears	Snow peas	Yams
Peas	Soy nuts	Yogurt
Pecans	Spinach	Zucchini
Peppers	Squash	
Persimmons	Strawberries	
Pineapple	String beans	

Stay active

Another way to keep your body healthy is to make sure it gets the activity it needs. Being active can improve your mood, energy, appearance, and sleep. It can also help to prevent or manage chronic problems like depression, diabetes, hypertension and heart disease.

The basics of exercise are simple: move your body and use your muscles. Consider your current activity level — are you moving enough?

Find a form of activity you enjoy. If you have exercise equipment, try using it while watching movies or favorite television shows. Listen to your favorite music or audio books while you exercise. Move in ways you enjoy — dance, swim, run, walk, play sports, do yoga or tai chi, bicycle, skate, ski or go to a gym.

The point is to take charge and be active, to keep moving instead of falling into an unhealthy, sedentary lifestyle.

What forms of exercise do you already enjoy?
_____
_____

What other ways of moving your body and using your muscles might you enjoy?
_____
_____

What specific things could you do to be more physically active, to move your body and use your muscles?
_____
_____

Sleep well

Sleep is important. Being deprived of good sleep can disturb your mood, energy, concentration and normal thought processes. Having a healthy and balanced lifestyle includes getting a good night's sleep on a regular basis.

Yet many people don't sleep well. Some have trouble getting to sleep; others wake up in the night and have difficulty getting back to sleep. Some wake up feeling unrested.

There are things you can try on your own to improve the quality of your sleep. Here are some basic guidelines for sleeping well:

- Go to sleep about the same time each night. A regular sleep pattern helps.
- Do something relaxing just before bedtime. Avoid stimulating activities.
- Use your bed for sleeping. Don't read, eat, watch TV or use electronics.
- Be careful about chemicals. Caffeine and other stimulants can keep you awake. Alcohol may help you fall asleep, but too much disturbs your sleep in the night.
- Don't lie in bed awake. If you're not asleep within 15-30 minutes, get up and do something else. Go back to bed when you feel sleepy.
- Finally, get up at about the same time each morning. Don't sleep in no matter how much you've been awake during the night. And don't nap during the day.

How would you rate the quality of your sleep in general?

_____
_____

What changes could you make to improve your sleep?

_____
_____

Consider medication

We live in a time when popping a pill is often the first thing recommended for coping with pain, emotional problems, insomnia or trouble concentrating. Pharmaceutical companies once marketed their medications to medical professionals. Now it's difficult to read a magazine or newspaper, watch TV or surf the Internet without coming across advertisements for medications to fix your depression, lower your cholesterol or solve your sexual problems. At a time when taking medication is the default response for almost any ailment, it's no surprise that some people also turn to alcohol and illicit drugs to cope with life's difficulties.

However, medications do have a place in self-management when they are used as prescribed under competent medical supervision. Let's take a look at the "What" and "When" of using medication for self-management.

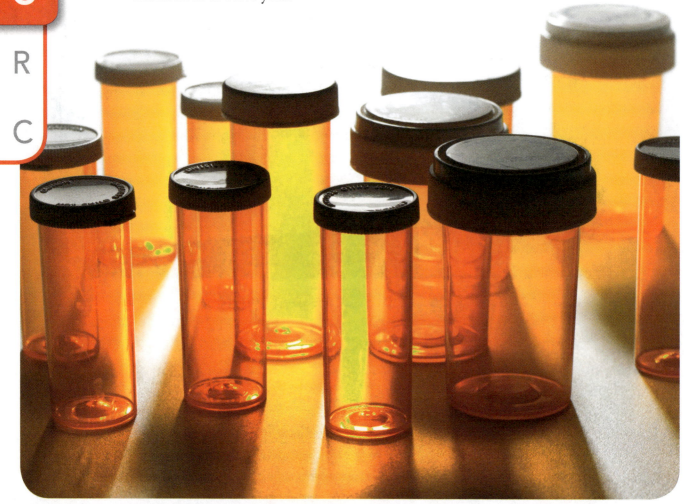

What medication should you consider?

You are probably familiar with medication to help improve your physical health such as when you take antibiotics to help fight bacterial infections.

You may also know there are many effective medications to help people cope with depression, anxiety, mood swings, sleep problems and cravings to use alcohol or other drugs.

These medications work by changing the balance of natural chemicals in the brain. Psychiatrists and other doctors can prescribe these medications, but it's important that you understand how they work and when to use them.

If you choose to take the medications recommended for you, you have a responsibility to yourself to help the medications do what they're supposed to do.

Be sure to take the correct dosage at the right times of day and for as long as prescribed. For some medications, it is particularly important to take the full amount for the full length of time recommended – don't just stop when you start feeling better.

Some medications come with specific instructions, such as to take them with food or to avoid certain things like alcohol, direct sunlight or driving or using heavy machinery while taking them. Read the instructions carefully.

What medications are you already taking (either prescription or over-the-counter)?

Medication Name	Daily Dose	Taken to Help With

When should you use medication?

In a life-threatening crisis or medical emergency, others may make a decision for you about which medication you need. Except in these emergency situations, consider the following questions when thinking about using medication:

1. Have you tried any nonmedication coping strategies before? What worked for you and what didn't?

2. Did you have significant psychological problems long before you developed problems with alcohol or other drugs? Or have you had mental health problems continue or get worse even when you were not using alcohol or other drugs for a period of weeks or months? If so, just getting free from alcohol/drug use is not likely to make these problems go away. It may be beneficial to consider medication in addition to counseling and behavior changes.

3. Did you start having mood swings, anxiety, depression, hallucinations or paranoid feelings only after developing alcohol/drug problems or addiction? Do these problems seem to happen only when you are intoxicated or withdrawing from alcohol/drug use? If so, it may make sense to hold off on trying other medications for these problems until you see whether they clear up again when you have quit or cut back on your alcohol/drug use. You can also learn other nonmedication coping strategies to help with these problems.

4. Do you now have both mental health and active substance use problems that are causing you distress? Usually it is best to treat both problems at the same time, whether using medication or other coping strategies to help resolve them.

Try biofeedback

Biofeedback is a way of learning how to make specific physical changes in your body when you want to. Research with biofeedback has shown that it is possible to learn self-control over body functions once thought to be beyond voluntary control.

A piece of biofeedback equipment measures a particular Organic function of the body and converts it into something you can see, hear or feel.

For example, there are biofeedback devices to measure your heart rate, skin temperature, tension in particular muscles and electrical brain waves. The machine might turn one of these, such as the alpha waves in your brain, into a tone you can hear. As you try to make the pitch go up or down, you learn how to increase this restful and peaceful form of electrical brain activity.

Biofeedback has been used successfully to help people learn how to relax muscle tension, reduce headaches, manage anxiety or pain and increase a drug-free sense of well-being. This approach, of course, requires the help of a professional with experience in biofeedback and the proper equipment.

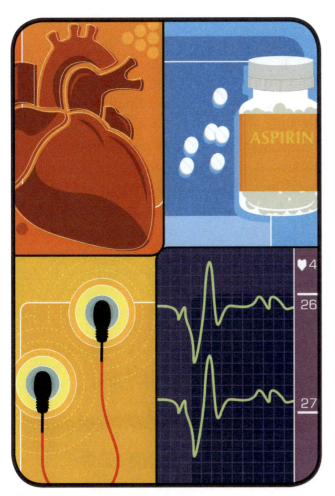

How might biofeedback be useful to you?
_____
_____

How might biofeedback help you reach your change goals?
_____
_____

Avoid alcohol
and other drugs

Finally, the state and well-being of your body are affected by drugs you put into it. The use of prescription medications was discussed earlier (pages 62-64).

To oversimplify, most drugs associated with problem use fall into one of three categories: Up, Down or Out. Uppers (such as caffeine, cocaine and methamphetamine) artificially increase heart rate, energy, concentration and a sense of well-being. Downers like alcohol and barbiturates depress or shut down body functions (including breathing and heart rate). "Outer" drugs like hallucinogens and cannabis directly alter thought and perception. Some drugs do more than one of these things. Opioids, for example, have both Down and Out functions – they depress heart rate and breathing while also altering mental processes. Most of these drugs also have additional and sometimes dangerous effects. Alcohol, for example, impairs judgment, perception, reaction time and coordination. It also tends to increase aggression and the misperception of social situations. While alcohol can make it easier to fall asleep, it also tends to disturb the quality of sleep and can cause nightmares and awakening in the night.

What negative effects (if any) do you suspect your own use of alcohol or other drugs has had on your body and physical wellness?

_____
_____
_____
_____

Change your responses

The preceding sections have focused on things you might consider and change with regard to your Situation, your Thinking and your Organic pattern – your mind and body. The fourth link in the STORC chain, R, is how you Respond, what you do, your behavior. It offers yet another place where it is possible to make positive changes.

How you Respond is a choice. If someone slaps you, do you strike back, "turn the other cheek" in some way or walk away? When you aren't getting what you want, do you angrily demand it and threaten, persistently ask for it or quietly give up? In every situation, many different Responses are possible, and what you choose to do is up to you. This section focuses on learning about and managing your own behavior, which is another form of self-control and self-determination.

Describe a Situation in which you could have made the wrong decision or might have responded badly, but instead you acted in a different way that turned out well.

What was the Situation?
_____
_____

What were you Thinking to yourself at the time?
_____
_____

How were you feeling at the time?
_____
_____

What might you have done (that could have resulted in a bad outcome)?
_____
_____

How did you actually Respond instead?
_____
_____

What happened as a Consequence? How did it turn out?
_____
_____

Become aware

One way to make a change in how you Respond is to start observing yourself by keeping track of what you do. The results can be surprising. Sometimes this alone helps you to change just by making you more aware. For example, if you wanted to change your diet and eat in a more healthy way, you could start keeping a diary of what you eat, like this:

	Su	Mo	Tu	We	Th	Fr	Sa	Total
Fruit servings								
Grain servings								
Meat and Bean servings								
Milk servings								
Vegetable servings								

Or suppose you wanted to improve your positive communication with someone you love. You may have decided that one good way to do this is to focus on saying positive, affirming things more often and negative, critical things less often. You might simply keep track of the number of positive (P) and negative (N) things you say to this person each day.

	Sunday	Monday	Tuesday	Wednesday	Thursday	Friday	Saturday
Positives	⊮ //						
Negatives	///						

This is just for your own information and awareness. You do not need to show it to anyone else, and you can track something secretly. Sometimes it is helpful to keep track for a week or two without trying to change anything so you have a clear starting point. This lets you keep a day-by-day and week-by-week score for yourself:

First Week

	Su	Mo	Tu	We	Th	Fr	Sa	Total
Positives	2	1	1	0	2	3	1	10
Negatives	12	8	14	6	10	8	11	69

What is a Response, a behavior of yours, you would like to increase or decrease?

_____
_____
_____
_____

Choose a behavior you can count. (See the change your diet and eat healthy example on page 68.) Customize the diary form below to help you keep track of what you do each week.

Week 1:

	Su	Mo	Tu	We	Th	Fr	Sa	Total
_____								
_____								
_____								
_____								

Week 2:

	Su	Mo	Tu	We	Th	Fr	Sa	Total
_____								
_____								
_____								
_____								

Take one step at a **time**

A big mistake people often make when trying to change is all-or-none Thinking. This is what tends to go wrong with New Year's resolutions. Consider the example: "I'm going to give up _____." Then comes the first violation of the rule. "Now I've blown it. I was going to give up _____, but now I went and did it. What's the use?" Thus fail the best of intentions.

When most people change successfully they do it bit by bit, a little at a time. Every step in the right direction is still progress, and a step back doesn't have to mean failure. If you want to make a big change, break it down (if you can) into smaller steps. Although you might have an ultimate change goal, like remembering to take an important medication on time every time, what would be a good small step in that direction?

That's why you need to know where you're starting from, so you know when you're making progress. Say it's a medication that you're supposed to take three times a day with meals. Start a first week diary before taking any active steps to change. Here's an example:

	Su	Mo	Tu	We	Th	Fr	Sa	Total
On time	1	2	2	1	1	1	2	10
Taken late	1	0	1	2	0	1	1	6
Missed completely	1	1	0	0	2	1	0	5

In the first week, just less than half of the pills were taken on time, plus six more taken late, and five skipped altogether. What would be a good goal for the next week as a step in the right direction?

_____ pills taken on time

_____ pills taken late

_____ pills missed

S T O R² C

Do something incompatible

If you're trying to decrease a "bad habit," one strategy is to do something else that is incompatible with that habit. For example, suppose you want to decrease your use of alcohol, perhaps with the ultimate goal of quitting completely.

What activities could you do that would make you unlikely to drink? You are essentially replacing one response with another. Here is a list you might make of situations in which you'd be unlikely to drink:

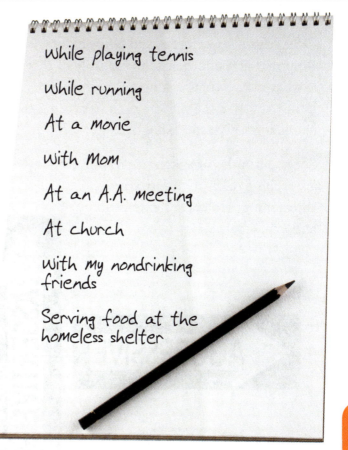

While playing tennis
While running
At a movie
With Mom
At an A.A. meeting
At church
With my nondrinking friends
Serving food at the homeless shelter

Think of a behavior you want to do less of in your life. What is this behavior?
_____

In what situations are you less likely to engage in this behavior?
_____
_____

With whom are you less likely to engage in this behavior?
_____   _____
_____   _____

Now think of things you do (or can do) that make you unlikely to engage in this behavior. List them here.
_____
_____
_____

Find a **middle** road

Often there is a middle road between one Response and another. One example of this is what is known as assertive responding. Being assertive is a middle path between being aggressive and being passive.

Some examples of aggressive responding are: yelling, blaming, criticizing, threatening, violence, name-calling and exploding.

Some examples of passivity are: saying nothing, giving in, giving up, stuffing your feelings, withdrawing, walking away, changing the subject and ignoring.

Some people think you have to do one or the other: strike out or walk away; threaten or give in; vent your feeling or stuff it. Assertive responding is a middle way between these two extremes.

The goal of aggression is, "I win, you lose."

The goal of assertiveness is win/win, "You matter and I matter. You count and I count."

The result of passivity is, "You win (at least for now) and I lose."

Situation: You would like to see a new movie and your partner would like to go dancing.

Aggressive: "We're going to the movie and that's final!"

Passive: "Okay (glumly), we'll go dancing instead."

Assertive: "Well, I really do want to see this movie, and you really want to dance. How about if we go to the movie and then go dancing afterward?"

Being assertive expresses your feelings and preferences without stepping on the other person's. "You count and I count."

> **Situation:** A woman feels jealous that her boyfriend kissed a pretty woman good-bye as they were leaving a party.
>
> **Aggressive:** "You jerk! What were you doing kissing her like that? Did you think I wouldn't notice? You never think about me!" [You're wrong, I'm right.]
>
> **Passive:** She says nothing about it. [My feelings don't matter.]
>
> **Assertive:** I felt really jealous when you kissed her. I like kissing you [You matter.] and I just hurt when I see you kissing someone else [and I matter]."

An assertive response is one that respects and honors the other person, and also respects and honors your own needs and desires.

> In your estimation, how often do you respond aggressively, assertively or passively? Divide up the circle below into three pie slices to show how often you are **aggressive (solid)**, **passive (white)** and **assertive (striped)**.

Example:

You:

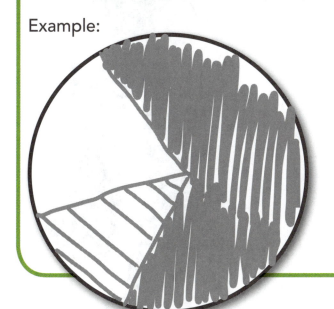

Listen

It is a gift to listen to someone. Many people pay a counselor or therapist just to have someone listen to them. Good listening strengthens relationships, builds friendships and prevents misunderstanding. It says to the other person, "You matter. You are important to me. I want to really understand what you are saying and feeling."

There are some basics to good listening:

1. **Pay attention.** Be "all ears." Don't be thinking of something else or of what you want to say next. Just listen. Usually this means keeping eye contact with the speaker (who will naturally look away and then back at you periodically). Don't be doing anything else while you're listening. Give the person your whole attention.

2. **Quiet your own stuff.** It's hard to be listening while you're talking. Good listening involves suspending, at least for the time being, your own material.

3. **Avoid roadblocks.** Here are some things that are not good listening:

   - Giving advice, suggestions or solutions
   - Warning or shaming
   - Agreeing or disagreeing
   - Asking a lot of questions
   - Judging or criticizing

Listen actively

So, what do you say instead of roadblocks? The skill here is called "active listening." Think about one single communication. Before speaking, the speaker has a meaning, something that she or he means to communicate (Box 1 in the drawing below). The speaker puts that meaning into words (Box 2), and of course people don't always say exactly what they mean.

Then you have to hear the words (Box 3). If you're not listening carefully, if it's noisy around you, you have a bad phone connection or if for some other reason you have trouble hearing, you may not get the words right.

Finally, you have to decide what you think the person means (Box 4).

All of this goes on constantly, often unconsciously, and most of the time, people respond as if what they think the person meant is what was actually meant. In other words, that Box 4 = Box 1.

But with every communication there are three places where it can go wrong:

- People don't say quite what they mean;
- You may not hear the words correctly; and
- You may guess wrong about the person's meaning.

Active listening is all about making sure that you got it right, that you understand. It is, in essence, checking Box 4 against Box 1.

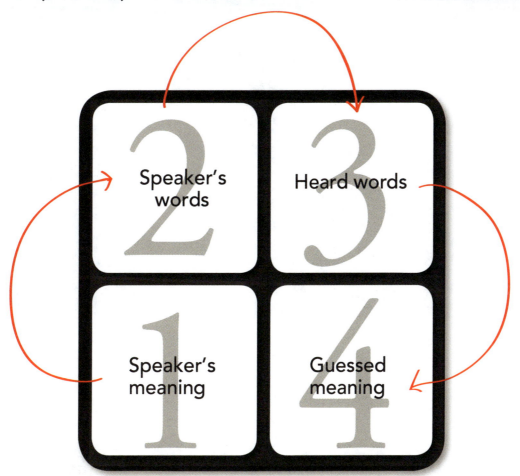

Listen (continued)

Good listening is actually a challenging skill that takes some time to learn. It is helpful to know some basics. First of all, it's not about asking questions. There is a natural tendency to ask, "Is this what you mean?" because basically that is what you are doing, but if you ask direct questions it starts to feel weird. For example:

- I'm exhausted today.
- Do you mean that you're physically tired?
- Yes, I didn't get much sleep last night.
- You mean you couldn't get to sleep?
- No, I woke up and couldn't get back to sleep.
- Are you saying that this happens to you often?
- Well, no.
- So what you're saying is that it doesn't happen very often?
- No, it doesn't.
- You mean last night was unusual then?
- Oh, never mind!

While it feels natural to you that you're trying to understand by asking questions, you may make the other person uncomfortable. It's just not normal conversation, and whenever you ask a question it puts pressure on the other person to answer. Questions are roadblocks. They can steer the person away from what he or she is trying to tell you, as happened above.

Good active listening is actually a *statement* about how you understand what the person means. It is a guess (Box 4) in the form of a statement about what the person means (Box 1). It is a reflection, a statement that reflects back to the person what you understand about his or her meaning.

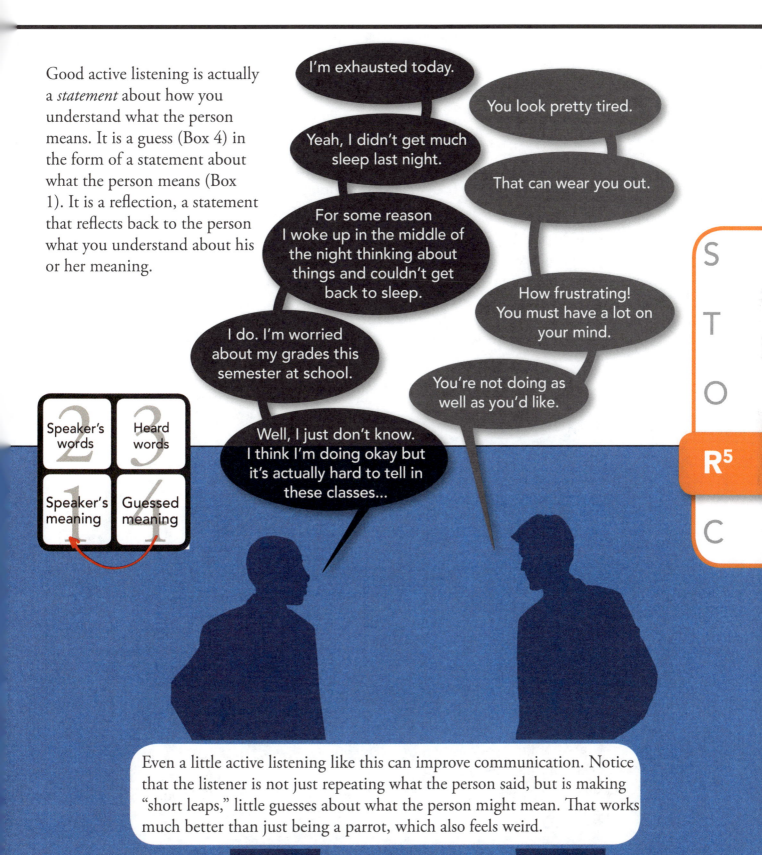

Even a little active listening like this can improve communication. Notice that the listener is not just repeating what the person said, but is making "short leaps," little guesses about what the person might mean. That works much better than just being a parrot, which also feels weird.

Learn from others

Most of the skills people acquire are learned by observing others. Imagine if each person had to rediscover, by trial and error on his or her own, all the steps involved in violin making, bread baking, playing the guitar, football or chess. Such skills are passed on from generation to generation by learners watching masters.

Here is another and perhaps quicker way to learn new skills. If you'd like to get better and more confident at social conversation, watch someone who is really good at it. What does this "master" do?

In Alcoholics Anonymous, newcomers are advised to work with a "sponsor" who has already been through the rough waters of early sobriety. Sponsors share the story of how they did it and offer practical advice based on what they have learned along the way.

What people do you know who are particularly good at a skill that you'd like to learn?

Person:_____ The skill:_____

Person:_____ The skill:_____

Person:_____ The skill:_____

- Mike keeps himself in terrific shape.
- Martha's willpower is really extraordinary.
- Rebecca is good at meeting new people and making friends.
- Jim always thinks things through before acting.
- Todd seems confident and sure of himself in every situation.
- Steve is a great listener.

Change your consequences

Now for the last link in the STORC chain, C, the Consequences of your actions. Perhaps these sound like they are beyond your control, but in fact there is much you can do here as well. These Consequences in turn become part of your ongoing Situation, and so the STORC cycle continues. Remember, the good news is that you can make changes at any link in the chain: S, T, O, R or C.

Choose your consequences

You can choose your Consequences by choosing your Responses wisely. There is a trap worth mentioning here. Sometimes people are told, "You can't..." and often it is not actually true. If a probation officer says, "You can't leave the city," it is not actually true. What it means is: "If you leave the city and get caught, there will be negative consequences." Similarly, people with alcohol use problems who are told, "You can't drink" know perfectly well that they can choose to do so. The meaning is that if they do drink, the results are likely to be negative.

The trap is that a person who is told, "You can't..." tends to experience resentment and a desire to say, "Oh yes I can!" Whenever someone claims to limit your choices, there is a natural reflex to assert your freedom. Even if you know very well the possible negative consequences, just being told, "You can't" may tempt you to prove that you can. A possible antidote thought here is: "I can, but I choose not to because..."

For example, a person with diabetes might be told, "You can't have sweets." A liberating thought is: "Actually, I can eat sweets; I just choose not to in the interest of my health."

What have you been told that you can't do? _____

_____

Is that actually true – that you are literally unable to do it? ___Yes   ___No

What do you feel or think when someone tells you that you can't do something?

_____

_____

Forks in the road

Each choice you make is like a fork in the road, where two paths diverge. Each path leads in a different direction, and you must choose one. Sometimes it is unclear where a particular choice will lead, but often you can make pretty good guesses.

Choosing your Consequences is about thinking through your options ahead of time, before you Respond. What are the different ways in which you could Respond, and what might be the Consequences of each? Here are two examples.

Situation: My boss asks me to work late again.

Response paths	Possible consequences
Path 1 (Aggressive) I refuse and say that I'm sick and tired of being asked to stay late.	I feel angry and resentful I lose my job
Path 2 (Assertive) I say that I have other plans and would really rather not, but if it's especially important I am willing to stay.	I feel good for expressing myself I improve the boss's attitude toward me Might not have to work late
Path 3 (Passive) I say nothing and stay late.	I have to work late I feel angry and resentful and show it

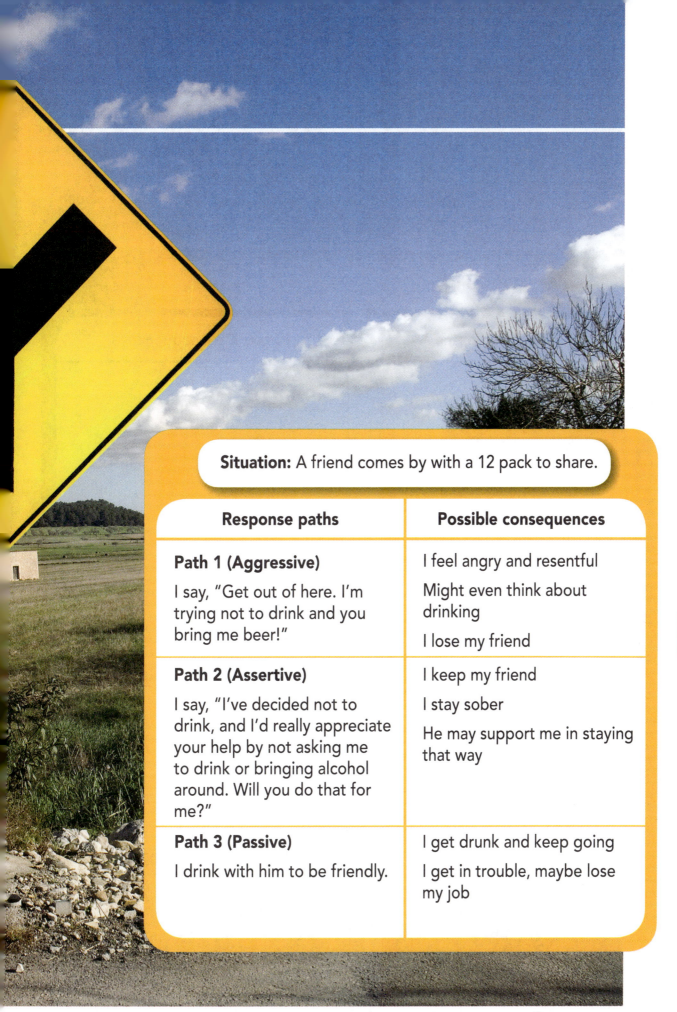

Situation: A friend comes by with a 12 pack to share.

Response paths	Possible consequences
Path 1 (Aggressive) I say, "Get out of here. I'm trying not to drink and you bring me beer!"	I feel angry and resentful Might even think about drinking I lose my friend
Path 2 (Assertive) I say, "I've decided not to drink, and I'd really appreciate your help by not asking me to drink or bringing alcohol around. Will you do that for me?"	I keep my friend I stay sober He may support me in staying that way
Path 3 (Passive) I drink with him to be friendly.	I get drunk and keep going I get in trouble, maybe lose my job

STORY

C¹

Forks in **your** road

What are some forks in the road that may lie ahead for you? Fill in the Situation, two or three possible choices you could make in how you Respond and what the Consequences of each might be.

Situation: _____

Response paths	Possible consequences
Path 1 (Aggressive) 	
Path 2 (Assertive) 	
Path 3 (Passive) 	

Situation: _____

Response paths	Possible consequences
Path 1 (Aggressive) _____ _____ _____ _____	_____ _____ _____ _____
Path 2 (Assertive) _____ _____ _____ _____	_____ _____ _____ _____
Path 3 (Passive) _____ _____ _____ _____	_____ _____ _____ _____

Reward yourself

It is a basic and obvious principle of human behavior that people are more likely to repeat Responses that have been rewarded in the past. If wearing one item of clothing gets you several compliments from friends and strangers, and wearing a different piece of clothing doesn't, you're more likely to wear the first piece of clothing again.

It is possible to reward yourself for making progress toward your goals if you follow one simple rule and stick to it:

When (and only when) I reach my next goal, I will reward myself by _____.

Until I reach that goal I will not reward myself in this way.

If you break this rule and reward yourself even if you don't reach your goal, it won't help. That would be like your boss saying, "I will pay you your salary whether or not you come to work and do your job."

What are good rewards to use for yourself? In general they should be:

- Small enough that they are realistic and easily available
- Enjoyable enough that you would work to get them
- Varied enough that you don't get tired of them
- Not harmful or self-defeating

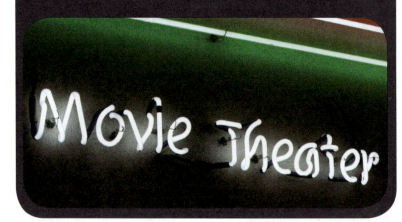

So what might be some good rewards that you would work for?

_____
_____
_____
_____

Kinds of rewards might include objects you buy, special food, going out, calling a friend, spending time with a friend, relaxing and doing things you particularly enjoy.

Here is another simple principle of learning. Suppose you have two things to do. One of these (X) you need to do, but don't particularly enjoy. The other (Y) is fun and you look forward to doing it. Which one should you do first?

The temptation is to do Y first because it's fun and allows you to put off the less enjoyable task. Of course, it is generally better to do X first and then do Y as a reward. This teaches you to get done what needs to be done before having fun.

Doing Y before X teaches you to put off what needs to be done (and perhaps not get it done well or at all).

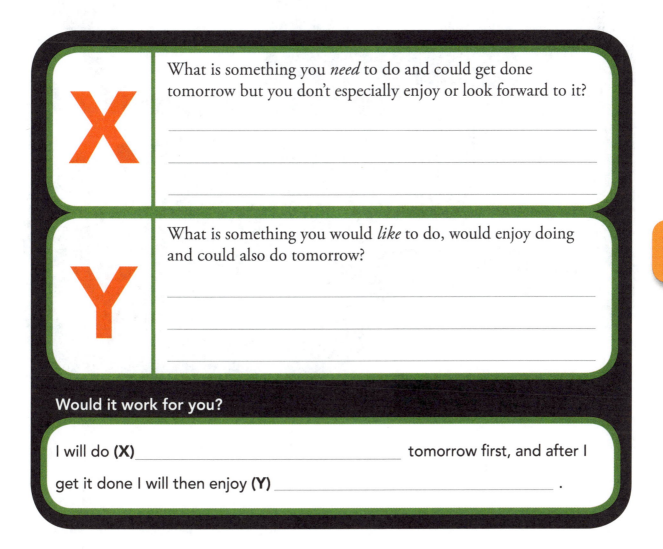

X — What is something you *need* to do and could get done tomorrow but you don't especially enjoy or look forward to it?

Y — What is something you would *like* to do, would enjoy doing and could also do tomorrow?

Would it work for you?

I will do (X) _____ tomorrow first, and after I get it done I will then enjoy (Y) _____ .

Celebrate with others

This is one common meaning of "self-control" – the ability to put off an immediate reward for a later or better one. Try an example:

Example:

You know how I enjoy it when you give me a back rub. You're so good at that. Well, I have a job I need to do, which is to get up on the roof and unclog the rain spouts.

It's a nasty job and I've been putting it off. After I've done it, would you massage my back? But only after I'm all done cleaning out the spouts.

Asking for the other person's help in this way increases your motivation.

Just letting someone else know what you intend to do increases your commitment to get it done.

When you do complete your task, there's a quick and simple reward – sharing a positive experience with someone. The shared reward might be going out for ice cream, having a dinner together, going to a movie or just relaxing together and talking.

What rewards could you share with someone else?

I could ask [person] _____ to celebrate with me by [activity] _____
_____

I could ask [person] _____ to celebrate with me by [activity] _____
_____

I could ask [person] _____ to celebrate with me by [activity] _____
_____

Use the space below to draw a situation like the example on page 86 where you are involving someone else in your change goals.

Put it all together

In this Journal you have encountered 29 different strategies for making changes in your life. Here they are again:

Change your SITUATION
1. Identify problem situations
2. Keep track
3. Avoid slippery places
4. Take along insurance
5. Change your environment
6. Ask others for help
7. Surround yourself with support

Change your ORGANIC PATTERNS
1. Relaxation
2. Stay active
3. Eat healthy
4. Sleep well
5. Consider medication
6. Try biofeedback
7. Avoid alcohol and other drugs

Change your THINKING
1. Become aware of troubling thoughts
2. Stop your thoughts
3. Reevaluate
4. Think positive
5. Try mental rehearsal
6. Coach yourself

Change your RESPONSES
1. Become aware
2. Take one step at a time
3. Do something incompatible
4. Find a middle road
5. Listen
6. Learn from others

Change your CONSEQUENCES
1. Choose your consequences
2. Reward yourself
3. Celebrate with others